SPEAKERS RESOURCE ORGANIZATION

Businesses Rely on Us...Audiences Remember Us!

Presents

Setting Effective Strategies:

Change, Preparing for Growth & People Power

Featuring:

Kristine Quade

Mary Henry

Jack Dermody

ISBN-13: 978-1493677818

ISBN-10: 1493677810

Published 2013

Created and Designed by ...
Be The Dream LLC

Publisher@BeTheDream.com

Want to spice up your next meeting?

Use a professional guest speaker from SRO.

The members of Speakers Resource Organization are seasoned professionals with a massive variety of industry backgrounds and expertise. They pride themselves in thought-provoking presentations and takeaways that land on your up-front-and-center bookshelf rather than a dark corner or round file.

Their clients -- corporations, non-profit groups, and business advisory groups -- repeatedly hire them for gold-standard facilitation and learning that sticks.

SRO delivers integrity with quality that exceeds client expectations. SRO is the vendor of choice for creating great events through information, sharing, and teaching.

Looking for a specific topic or timeframe? Let SRO assist you with either -- made-to-order for your event.

Contact info: info@speakersresourceorganization.com or any of the speakers presenting at today's event.

Table of Contents

ACCOMPLISHING WHAT OTHERS SAY IS IMPOSSIBLE

Dr Kristine Quade, EdD, JD, MSOD
E-Mail: Kristine@KristineQuade.com
Phone: 612-860-5992
http://wwwDynamicalLeadership.com

Events over the past few years have shown that in uncertain times, prediction and control are illusions in today's changing environment. Leaders who are able to see and influence competitive patterns are able to balance between data and intuition, planning and acting, safety and risk--all while giving due honor to each. Dr Quade will show you how to leverage your organization's strengths in alignment with a shifting competitive market place.

BACKDROP

FACT 1: You cannot always predict or control what happens in a complex system.

FACT 2: You cannot re-allocate your resources as fast as you need to when it is urgent.

FACT 3: Emerging markets are no longer providing low-cost skilled labor.

FACT 4: Collaborative efforts are not producing the necessary results for contributing partners.

FACT 5: You are still responsible to take wise action (or as wise as you can manage)

Given these FACTS, what are your options for action?

CONSIDERATIONS

Why do you Plan?

- To prepare for the future
- To coordinate action
- To reduce anxiety
- To avoid known risks
- To optimize known benefits
- To prepare for the future

    For the present, anyway.

What is the Problem?

- Do you really know what will happen?
- With whom and how?
- To avoid known risks?
- What about the unknown ones?
- To optimize known benefits?
- What about the unknown ones?
- Which future?

_____

_____

_____

_____

_____

_____

_____

_____

Accomplishing What Others Say Is Impossible

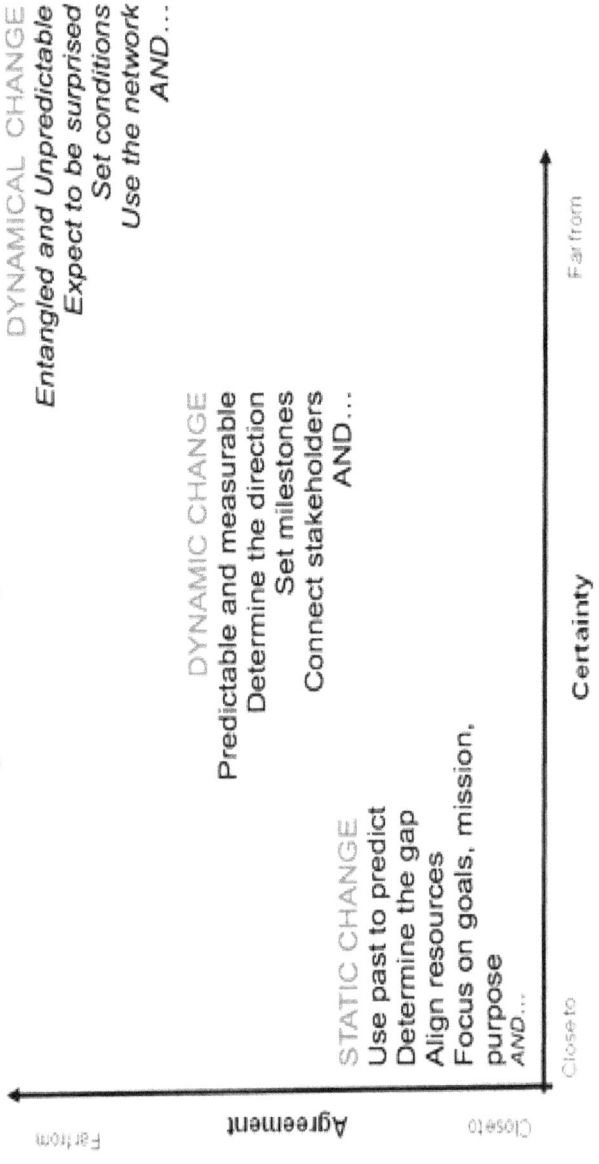

STATIC CHANGE
Use past to predict
Determine the gap
Align resources
Focus on goals, mission, purpose
AND...

DYNAMIC CHANGE
Predictable and measurable
Determine the direction
Set milestones
Connect stakeholders
AND...

DYNAMICAL CHANGE
Entangled and Unpredictable
Expect to be surprised
Set conditions
Use the network
AND...

Agreement

Certainty

Close to

Far from

Close to

Far from

THREE TYPES OF STRATEGY AND CHANGE

Static Change:

Little movement--like rocking a car to get out of a snow drift

- Use the past to predict.
- Determine the gap.
- Consider resistance.
- Figure out where to apply pressure.
- Don't get distracted by new information.
- Align resources.
- Focus on goal/mission, purpose.
- If it doesn't move, push harder.

What are you experiencing here?

_____

_____

_____

_____

_____

_____

_____

_____

_____

_____

_____

_____

Dynamic Change:

Predictable and measurable; expect future as continuation of the past.

- Determine the direction.
- Consider persistent forces.
- Figure out where to apply pressure.
- Set milestones.
- Connect with stakeholders.
- Focus on process and procedure.
- If it doesn't move in the right direction, find the culprit.

What are you experiencing here?

_____

_____

_____

_____

_____

_____

_____

_____

_____

_____

_____

_____

_____

_____

_____

_____

Dynamical Change:

Entangled and Unpredictable

- Expect to be surprised.
- Set conditions.
- Consider conditions for self-organizing.
- Figure out how to notice weak signals.
- Celebrate change at any scale.
- Use your network.
- Focus on part, whole, and greater whole.
- If it doesn't change, keep shifting conditions.

What are you experiencing here?

_____
_____
_____
_____
_____
_____
_____
_____
_____
_____
_____
_____
_____
_____
_____
_____
_____
_____

TWO WAYS TO THINK OF STRATEGY

Finite Boundaries	Infinite Boundaries
Defined field of play	Fuzzy boundaries
Opponents are known	Everybody plays
Rules are constant	Changing rules
Expertise is clear	Looking for fit
Been there before	New territory
Easy to keep score	Everything may matter
Purpose: To Win	*Purpose: Keep Playing*

QUESTIONS TO ASK TO SHIFT THE STRATEGY

What?
- Is the nature of change you face today?
- Have you done to plan in the past—what worked?

So what?
- Are the patterns of this change?
- Are your options if you see it as:
  - Static?
  - Dynamic?
  - Dynamical?

Now what?
- Will you plan in ways that fit and influence your reality?
- What will you do to prepare for the next cycle?

Your Questions

EXAMPLES

For the Entrepreneur

What?

What are current patterns and how are they serving?

What gaps exist to be filled?

What resources do I/my network have?

_____
_____
_____
_____
_____

So what?

So what unique contributions can I make?

So what risks are inherent?

So what risks am I ready to take?

_____
_____
_____
_____
_____

Now what?

Now what can I do?

Now what should I communicate and to whom?

Now what will I look for and when/how will I look?

_____
_____
_____
_____
_____
_____

For Leadership Capacity:

What?

What within my system are the pockets of predictability, reliability, stability or control and how is that serving or hindering me?

What does it look like when I seize the opportunity to explore, be creative or thrive in new insights?

How and from whom do I collect intelligence?

_____
_____
_____
_____
_____

So what?

So what helps me make meaning in my system?

So what is missing from important data?

So what might be happening with emergent ideas, the pace of learning, or candid conversations?

_____
_____
_____
_____
_____

Now what?

Now what actions do I need to take to make a difference here and now?

_____
_____
_____
_____
_____

ALIGNMENT. ENGAGEMENT. IMPLEMENTATION

An Introduction to the 7 Stages of Enterprise Growth

MARY HENRY

HR ON DEMAND LLC

MARY@HRONDEMANDLLC.COM

623-692-9213

Case Study

- Identify the stages of growth

- Outcomes from understanding

- Gates of focus

- Faces of the leader

- Builder vs Protectors

The 7 Stages of Entrepreneurial Growth

Stage 1	1-10	Start up
Stage 2	11-19	Ramp up
Stage 3	20-34	Delegation
Stage 4	35-57	Professional
Stage 5	58-95	Integration
Stage 6	96-160	Strategic
Stage 7	161 500	Visionary

What stage are you? _____

How do you know? _____

What evidence backs you up? _____

_____

_____

Outcomes from Understanding –
Your Company's Stage of Growth

- Help gain clarity of where a company is today and why the company may be experiencing specific growth issues

- Alignment of management team which allows issues to be identified and addressed sooner

- Look behind, examine today and look ahead to see what's creating obstacles to growth

- Help create a language of growth that will resonate with every single person in the company

_____

_____

_____

_____

_____

_____

_____

_____

The Rules That Govern the 7 Stages of Growth

- The movement from one stage of growth to another begins as soon as you land in any stage of growth.

- What you don't get done in a specific stage of growth does not go away.

- Time will make a difference.

- If you aren't growing, you are dying.

_____

_____

_____

_____

_____

_____

Three gates of focus

Profit/Revenue Gate

Predicting growth by maximizing and anticipating profit and revenue, protection and capacity issues

People Gate

Building competency and innovation through the conscious development of people

Process Gate

Transforming complexity into clarity through systems

_____

_____

_____

_____

_____

_____

_____

_____

What Are the Three Faces –

What Face Are You Wearing Today?

Visionary: Can take the most insignificant situation and turn it into an opportunity.

Manager: Creates order and focuses on the pragmatic systems and procedures that make the company run well.

Specialist: Is action oriented and detail focused, driven to complete tasks and centers on results, not ideas.

_____

_____

_____

_____

_____

Builders and Protectors:
Which One Are You Today?

Builders: A Builder mindset creates new ideas, takes on new initiatives, and finds ways to expand the revenue and profitability of the enterprise. They are risk tolerant and highly supportive of growth.

Protectors: A Protector mindset is cautious and prefers to slow things down. They are risk averse and highly suspicious of growth.

_____

_____

_____

_____

_____

_____

_____

_____

How will you manage your growth?

_____

_____

_____

_____

_____

_____

_____

_____

_____

_____

A GREAT BOARD OF DIRECTORS FOR EVEN THE SMALLEST BUSINESS

Jack Dermody
Email: dermody@cox.net
Phone: (602) 317-9707
Website: http://www.JackDermody.com

STRATEGIC THINKING

Percentage of the world's population that thinks strategically: 10%

Sample Corporate Positions Held by Strategic Thinkers

- Most C-Level positions
- Planning
- Market analysis
- Financial analysis
- Sales projections
- Technology
- Product development
- IT

Core Values of Strategic Thinkers

- Knowledge and competence with big-picture systems
- Efficiency
- Pure logic and love of abstract thinking

Business Strengths of Strategic Thinkers

- The long-term is priority
- Logic and objectivity
- Repeated success
- Utilitarian: Do what needs to be done

Where to Find Strategic Thinkers

- Professional C-Level advisors
- CEOs
- Sales and marketing heads
- Internet and social media experts
- Lawyers, doctors
- Know-it-all customers

Which Strategic Thinkers Are In Your Neighborhood to Call?

- SCORE
- Brother-in-law (or Sister-in-law) with big-picture reputation
- Head of sales where you bought your car
- Your website designer
- Your attorney, doctor (specialist)
- Customers who ask the hardest questions

ACTION QUESTIONS FOR YOU

1. Who do you know that you can call for this kind of thinking?

2. How will you work with them for maximum impact?

3. What will attract them to work with you?

    a. What activities *naturally* turn them on...or off?
    b. What's in it for them?
    c. What are you willing and able to do for them?
    d. How else might you work together inside and outside of business?

NOTES

_____
_____
_____
_____
_____
_____

LOGISTICAL THINKING

Percentage of the world's population that thinks logistically: 45%

Sample Corporate Positions Held by Logistical Thinkers

- Accounting
- Purchasing
- Facilities
- Engineering
- Manufacturing
- Inspection
- Distribution

Core Values of Logistical Thinkers

- Responsibility
- Rules, policies, procedures
- Doing the right thing
- Cooperation
- Concrete thinking -- feel planted in the real world

Business Strengths of Logistical Thinkers

- Rule-orientation
- Restraint
- Correct and careful processing
- Patience, persistence, willingness to plod
- Traditional beliefs

Where to Find Logistical Thinkers

- Operations managers
- Financial advisors
- Tax accountants
- Engineers
- Bankers, lenders, creditors
- Members of traditional clubs, e.g., Rotary
- Anal-retentive customers

Which Logistical Thinkers Are In Your Neighborhood to Call?

- SCORE
- Accountants
- Financial advisors
- Bankers and creditors
- Logistics-oriented business friends
- Friends in traditional clubs
- Customers who seem worried about everything

ACTION QUESTIONS FOR YOU

1. Who do you know that you can call for this kind of thinking?
2. How will you work with them for maximum impact?
   a. What activities *naturally* turn them on...or off?
   b. What's in it for them?
   c. What are you willing and able to do for them?
   d. How else might you work together inside and outside of business?

NOTES

_____
_____
_____
_____
_____
_____
_____
_____
_____
_____
_____
_____
_____
_____
_____
_____

TACTICAL THINKING

Percentage of the world's population that thinks tactically: 30%

Sample Corporate Positions Held by Tactical Thinkers

- Sales
- Negotiating
- Retail
- Marketing
- Design
- Art
- Event coordination

Core Values of Tactical Thinkers

- Personal freedom
- Living solidly in the now
- Thinking concretely
- Direct, efficient goal attainment

Business Strengths of Tactical Thinkers

- Physical: hands-on, real-world, and concrete
- Immediate-action orientation
- Fast action
- High creativity
- Knowing "cool" from stodgy
- Adventure, risk

Where to Find Tactical Thinkers

- People who sell expensive things
- People who think on their feet, e.g., courtroom attorneys
- Entrepreneurs not located in an office
- Financially successful people despite " impulsivity rep"
- Customers needing fast, easy service

Which Tactical Thinkers Are In Your Neighborhood to Call?

- Car sales people and the backroom guys
- Your son's coach
- Sales people of all kinds
- Multi-taskers who seem to make money no matter what they touch
- Your most impatient customers

ACTION QUESTIONS FOR YOU

1. Who do you know that you can call for this kind of thinking?
2. How will you work with them for maximum impact?
3. What will attract them to work with you?
   a. What activities *naturally* turn them on...or off?
   b. What's in it for them?
   c. What are you willing and able to do for them?
   d. How else might you work together inside and outside of business?

NOTES

_____
_____
_____
_____
_____
_____
_____
_____
_____
_____
_____
_____
_____
_____
_____

DIPLOMATIC THINKING

Percentage of world's population that thinks diplomatically: 15%

Sample Corporate Positions Held by Diplomatic Thinkers

- C-level of Non-Profit Organizations
- Public relations
- Customer service
- HR
- Training
- Wellness
- Community outreach

Core Values of Diplomatic Thinkers

- Harmonic relationships
- Cooperation
- Empathy
- Openness to endless ideas

Business Strengths of Diplomatic Thinkers

- People orientation
- Conflict resolution
- Networking
- Future orientation
- Idea processing

Where to Find Diplomatic Thinkers

- People great with customers
- Public relations experts
- Excellent connectors in social media
- Teambuilders
- Wellness experts
- Community supporters
- Trainers, teachers, facilitators, counselors, therapists

Which Diplomatic Thinkers Are In Your Neighborhood to Call?

- Your most approachable friends for small talk and socializing
- Social media experts
- Community volunteers
- HR managers, especially in wellness and training

ACTION QUESTIONS FOR YOU

1. Who do you know that you can call for this kind of thinking?
2. How will you work with them for maximum impact?
3. What will attract them to work with you?
   a. What activities *naturally* turn them on...or off?
   b. What's in it for them?
   c. What are you willing and able to do for them?
   d. How else might you work together inside and outside of business?

NOTES

_____
_____
_____
_____
_____
_____
_____
_____
_____
_____
_____
_____
_____
_____
_____
_____
_____
_____

10 Darn Good Reasons to Invite Jack to Your Workplace

1. Your budget can handle Jack because…he has a program for **every budget**.
2. You want your people to work together **a whole lot better**.
3. Communication could be **a whole lot better**.
4. Conflict could happen **a whole lot less**.
5. Jack's lessons **stick** after he's gone.
6. Your company's culture could be **smarter, more efficient, faster, and friendlier.**
7. People of **all** education levels "get" Jack's lessons.
8. Try his **Four Windows program** first. It breaks the ice. Not everybody says Four Windows is miraculous, but some do. You just might too!
9. All participants get easy-to-use **tools** to use **for life**.
10. Expect your **culture to change** for the far better.

A Testimonial

"Wow! From the moment you walk in to one of Jack Dermody's Four Windows workshops, you know things are going to be different. Our group was animated, laughing, and thoroughly enjoying learning about their own personality survey as well as that of the other teammates. I had no idea Oprah Winfrey had the same temperament that I have! We learned how to influence others in positive, productive ways as well as increase team cooperation -- great skill sets anyone can benefit from. Jack Dermody's presentation is dynamic, engaging, and very informative. We can't wait to have him come back and share one of his other workshops with our facilitators. Thanks Jack!"
         - Carrie Cohill, Arizona Association of Facilitators

Our Next Taster...

Negotiating Conflict in Business and Personal Relationships

Are you being held hostage by conflict? Do you wish you could break free from certain clients or relationships that are causing difficulty? What are your weak areas that cause you to clash with other personality styles? This program will provide you with effective tools that can be used immediately to improve your interpersonal communication skills and your bottom line.

Within this presentation you will learn:

- How to harness your own power to face difficult situations.

- How to diffuse conflict immediately at home and at work

- What is authentic leadership?

- Five styles for responding to conflict

- How to "fire" a problematic client and keep the relationship

- How to use the energy generated from conflict for success

Wednesday, March 26

9 AM to 10:30 AM

Check our website for more details and location.

www.SpeakersResourceOrganization.com

Meet Our Presenters

SPEAKERS RESOURCE ORGANIZATION

Bruce Benefiel

Bruce 'Zen' Benefiel, Founder/Owner and Chief Possibilities Coagulator at Be The Dream, LLC, is an author, speaker on holistic systems, project planning and self-development. He was blessed with the ability to say yes, take risks and garner worlds of experience and success across several industries. His forte: putting people, places and things together to do amazing stuff. He's also helped many authors become self-published through his expertise in journalism and self-publishing.

A highly qualified educator and facilitator, his presentations are engaging, intelligent, timely and witty. His passion is personal development and self-awareness that leads to making sense common – the foundation for any endeavor or project. His expertise also includes facilitating 'partnering' workshops for large concerns – building, road and bridge construction to name a few – under the Team Partnering LLC banner. Want a quick paradigm shift? Ask him how 'Zen' happened.

Hot Topics:

The Shift: Challenge to Change: *Removing Liabilities, Limitations and Excuses*

- Brilliant Behaviors that Work to Increase Performance
- Relation-ships on the Ocean of Emotion and How To Sail Them
- Three Elements that Connect Everyone to All Things Productive
- Best Practices for Connecting & Follow Up Exercises to Stay Fit

Growing Your Dream w/ Social Media - *Mania to Metanoia*

- Metanoia – A Change of Mind that Gets Results
- Definition of Social Media & Resources, Strategies and Tactics
- What Social Media Can Do For You and HOW TO Do It
- Pitfalls of Poor Media and Relationship Management

Communication and Problem-Solving - Keys to Partnering

- Practicing the Principles of Partnering – Commitment, Communication, Integrity and Trust
- Creating a Charter/Mission with Goals and Objectives that are Measurable
- Teamwork and Responsibility in the Process of Issue Resolution
- Tools for Effective Communication that Empowers Excellence

New Millennial Business Management Models - *Making Sense Common*

- What is a New Millennial Mindset and Why Would I Want One?
- Holistic Systems Approach to Understanding Flow and Productivity
- Transparency without Travesty – Doing the Right Things Right
- Aspirations for Excellence to Creating an Action Plan that Achieves

10 Steps to Growing Your Business in Good or Bad Times - *An Holistic Approach*

- Sales and Customer Statistical Awareness – What's Your Number?
- Enhancing the Customer Experience – Customer-Centric Tactics
- Use of Technology Beyond the Distractions and Interruptions
- Creating a Culture & Community that Thrives in Today's Market

Susan Bulfinch

 Susan Bulfinch, with over 25 years' experience in mediation and conflict resolution, is a professional *neutral* in private practice mediating family, employment, sexual harassment, commercial, small business, and real estate matters.

Susan mediates for the United States Postal Service REDRESS Program, Maricopa County Justice Courts and the Employment Mediation Panel for the American Arbitration Association. As an educator, Susan has lectured extensively on alternative dispute resolution and teaches two courses each spring at the University of California, Santa Barbara.

A graduate of Hampshire College and Southwestern University School of Law, Susan is past president of the Southern California Mediation Association, Arizona Association for Conflict Resolution, Maricopa County Association of Family Mediators and Metropolitan Business and Professional Women.

Hot Topics:

Mediation Skills for the Workplace

- Introduction of the mediation process and how it is used in the workplace
- Practice active listening and other communication tools
- Tips for creating an in-house mediation program

Got Conflict?   5 styles for responding to conflict

- Cost of conflict in the workplace
- Understanding your personal style: accommodating, competing, compromising, avoiding and collaborating
- Identify which style is appropriate for a given situation

You have a choice: Mediate – Don't Litigate

- Understand differences between mediation, arbitration and litigation
- Principles of mediation: neutral, confidential, voluntary
- Benefits of using mediation to improve communication and productivity

Beyond Reason: Understanding Emotions in Negotiation

- Identify 5 core concerns: appreciation, affiliation, autonomy, status, role
- Application of core concerns to a negotiation
- Negotiation tips

Dr. Richard Deems

Richard S Deems, PhD, has been quoted in Wall Street Journal, New York Times, Atlanta Journal-Constitution, CNBC News, CareerBuilder, The Ladders, Monster.com and even The Sporting News. He is the author of 12 books on key management issues, and co-author with his daughter Terri A Deems, PhD, of the 5-Star books Leading In Tough Times and Make Job Loss Work For You.

Deems is founding president of WorkLife Design, with offices in Arizona, Iowa, and Illinois. WorkLife Design works in all segments of the economy, including finance, insurance, manufacturing, retail, higher education, non-profits, and healthcare. Their client's revenues range from $5M to $40B.

A popular speaker, Deems has presented more than 2,000 keynotes, executive seminars, and workshops from coast to coast. He's presented at ASTD Regional, International, and Leadership Conferences, and consistently receives high evaluations. One participant reported, "Didn't get my afternoon nap," and another said, "We got more than our money's worth."

Hot Topics:

- **Taking Care of Your Own Career**

- **How to Turn Job Hunting into Job Getting**

- **High Performance – Doing What Comes Naturally**

- **Why Everyone Doesn't React to Change the Same Way**

- **Crush the Biggest Mistake Executives Make**

- **Putting the Right Person in the Right Seat In the…**

- **Developing Support for Change When the Stakeholders Didn't Create It**

Jack Dermody

Jack Dermody (UCLA, MA) has worked to advance human communication and personal relationships for thirty years through language and psychology. He is a corporate trainer, group facilitator, and consultant.

Beyond Four Windows temperament creations, he lights fires under teams and demonstrates effective communication, actual conflict management, and personal development. His clients include corporations and government organizations on five continents.

Interesting career notes.

- Created the prized Four Windows Personality Survey
- Writes the weekly newsletter "Personality Matters"
- Is in high-demand as a corporate facilitator
- Founded the Speakers Resource Organization (SRO)
- Was Curriculum and Training Coordinator for the City of Phoenix;
- Wrote 13 books on language learning
- Headed marketing and sales for international publisher
- Began his career in the Peace Corps in West Africa

Hot Topics:

SATISFY 4 TYPES OF PROSPECTS TO CLOSE MOST SALES: How Personality-Driven Companies Rule the Marketplace

- The Types: The Careful, The Impulsive, The Idealistic, The Expert
- The "personality" of your product matters
- Your style of communication counts more than you may know
- Examples abound of major-league, personality-driven companies

HIRE YOUR WEAKNESSES AND WIN: Acknowledging a Need for Help Trumps Staying Stupid (...and Mediocre)

- Identifying and living with your deficits
- Delegating with skill and joy
- Leveraging your strengths
- Dominating the marketplace

SURE, BUILD YOUR TEAM, BUT MOVE THEM TO <u>ACT</u>: Teams Need a Leader with Persuasive Skills

- Calling a group of people a team does not make them a team
- Who are your leaders? What are their significant strengths and costly weaknesses?
- Persuasion is a skill that everybody can learn
- By demanding persistent action, you never settle for second-rate

MANAGE CONFLICT BY CREATING A CULTURE OF PERSONALITIES: It's Hard to Get Mad When You Quickly Assess Where People Are Really Coming From

- Choosing temperament assessment tools that balance the playing field for Harvard graduates and high school dropouts
- Understanding self and (almost) all others
- Changing communication in the whole organization in days or weeks
- Making positive, authentic changes and keeping them on the front burner forever

IS YOUR WELLNESS PROGRAM SAVING YOU HEALTH INSURANCE MONEY? The Only Fitness Program That Works Is the One That Will Cater to Individual Styles

- Healthcare insurance companies want to reward low-risk fitness
- Getting fit and staying fit is difficult and complex at every levels
- Competent education and training cost far less than the premiums you are paying now
- Real fitness happens when people know their real selves and what is really possible

Valerie Harper

 Valerie Harper is creator/owner of True Wealth Consulting. She offers private consultations, group lectures and has authored 24 books on navigating the inner self. She writes screenplays and specializes in assisting people put together their personal stories so they can better understand their psychology so they can live with better love, harmony, vibrant health and prosperity.

"As a true wealth consultant I assist people in removing their inner obstacles to getting what they want. There are many different approaches to wellness that no longer takes 20 years of therapy. My work is based on a new approach to psychological design. What people used to cope with now stops them from living with authentic fulfillment and success. Each presentation is designed to cultivate a deeper sense of inner awareness to help you thrive in a specific way." –Valerie Harper

Main Topics for Presentations Include:

- Calculating Your Wealth Formula

- The Abundance of Self

- The Tao of Alternative Healing

- Emotional Traumas that Lead to Poverty

- The Love Veteran's Relationship Course on Unrequited Love

Mary Henry

Mary Henry, President and Founder of HR on Demand, a business consulting firm that specializes in adding bottom line value to organizations through business development and sound human resource practices. Her company was founded in 2009, and serves business' of all sizes throughout the metro Phoenix area.

Prior to founding her own company, Mary spent 10+ years at a Fortune 50 company, serving in roles such as training and development, recruiting, employee relations, people development and various other projects and disciplines throughout the organization.

She has both small business and the large corporate experience. She holds the SPHR, Senior Professional in Human Resource designation from the Society of Human Resource Management.

Hot Topics:

How to get the most from your team and retain top talent.

Objectives of the program:

- Define engagement and the business case for doing so.
- How to provide feedback
- Performance management templates and tools

Unemployment: How to manage the process and claims.

Objectives of the program

- Program Guidelines
- Tax and Work Programs
- Best practices to avoid turnover

NLRB and unfair labor practices

- Identify the agencies governing employee rights.
- Determine the scope of their jurisdiction in employee relations issues
- Employee rights under these statutes
- Employer rights under these statutes
- Tools and tips for good employee relations

Minimizing turnover through effective sourcing, interviewing, assessing, and hiring.

- Understand how candidates search for jobs
- The impact of competency based interview questions
- When and how to administer pre-employment assessments

Allan Himmelstein

With a 30+ year track record of driving multimillion dollar revenue growth Allan Himmelstein is a trusted advisor and decisive sales leader. His extensive business management experience includes the startup of an international company, which grew to $40,000,000 in nine years, and serving as VP of Sales and Marketing for a $50,000,000 ConAgra company. Allan's expertise includes:

- Tactical sales and Marketing Planning
- Hiring the best sales and sales management for your particular need
- Best practices for managing, measuring, and motivating a sales force
- Sales coaching and mentoring.

Hot Topics:

Getting In the Door Without Cold Calling

We are all Accidental Sales People, and every business needs to sell. Learn proven sales strategies for getting in the door even if you have never sold before and without cold calling.

Handling the Appointment and Getting the Sale

The shortest Sales course in the world is "Ask Questions and Listen". However there is a process and a method to asking the right questions that eventually lead to a sale. This workshop will increase your opportunities to open new business.

10 Biggest Mistakes of Sales Managers

How many times have you heard, "My Salespeople Can't Sell?" Have we hired correctly? Have we given them the right tools? Have we made them into clerks or customer sales representatives? These answers and more will be covered, discussed, with some suggested solutions.

Karen Laughlin

 Karen Laughlin, SPHR, started Thomas Resources to develop leaders and provide opportunities for diverse professionals. Karen is a human capital specialist with over a decade of talent acquisition strategy, delivery and retention program experience with Fortune 100 companies.

Program management, executive coaching on talent strategies and project management of national recruiting events are additional accomplishments during her career. Karen naturally excels at building and maintaining valuable relationships with clients by listening to needs, identifying common ground and providing targeted solutions. Raised in a military family and living in multi-cultural environments developed Karen's passion for inclusion and the work of diversity.

Hot Topics:

American Values in the Workplace

During this session we will reminisce about the good old days in our organizations then consider our responsibility to maintain the American culture of leadership, innovation and excellence of being #1!

Specifically we'll review the following values and their impact on business performance and effective people resource management:

- Accountability
- Responsibility
- Engagement
- Performance excellence

Customer focused orientation (internal and external)

Career Management: Different outcomes for men and women

Career advancement strategies for women based on the recent Catalyst report "The Myth of the Ideal Worker: Does Doing all the Right Things Really Get Women Ahead?"

- Use information from this report to manage the career advancement of ourselves or of individuals who report to us
- Review factors that impact gender pay disparities
- Career Management impact on promotions, pay increases & job satisfaction

Social Media: Your personal Career Assistant

Social Media is free, always open and offers new resources daily. Learn how to launch then navigate these resources to land your next great job by connecting with people in the real world!

- Review current job search & unemployment trends
- Learn how and why to become a social media voyeur on… LinkedIn - Google+ - Twitter - Pinterest - Facebook
- Actions that lead to influential connections and securing interviews
- Extra Credit – Use social media to establish/brand yourself as a subject matter expert in your respective field

Motivation: The Key to making better people decisions

Regardless if we're hiring or identifying strategic partners to meet client expectations, being aware of individuals' motivations & values will enable you to make better choices, minimize risk, reduce problems & waste of valuable resources.

- Discover the components to identify, confirm and analyze potential partner's motivation thru questions, active listening & analysis
- Create a process map to improve the decisions made about staff or partners

Dr. Kristine Quade

Dr Kristine Quade focuses on accomplishing what others say is impossible. Keenly aware of the accelerating dynamics of uncontrollable change, Kristine has developed creative solutions for identifying the difference that makes a difference and guiding actions that are both flexible and realistic.

Her area of expertise includes leadership, global strategic thinking, creativity and innovation, team effectiveness and influencing the dynamics of discontinuous change.

Key Accomplishments:

- Worked with over 150 client systems in over 20 countries
- Author of 5 books and numerous articles on change
- Attorney and Doctorate in Organizational Change
- Founder of the Dynamical Leadership Academy
- Frequent keynote presenter at management conferences

Areas of Expertise:

Leadership, Organizational and Personal Effectiveness, Dynamics of Change

Hot Topics:

Simple Rules: The Leaders Guide to Navigating Unpredictable Change

- What creates the bond that holds members of a unit in coordinated action?
- What rallies individuals around a common cause?
- What guides individuals to make good decisions during a crisis?

The answer is in the concept of simple rules that find a balance between data and intuition, planning and acting, safety and risk, autonomy and control, and change and stability.

What the Bleep Do We Know About Change?

- Mechanistic approaches to change are no longer working.
- Complexity of change is magnifying what is broken.
- Unpredictability creates tension to over-correct

Want to understand the complex dynamics of change in a meaningful way? Want to become more resilient when needing to adapt? Want to identify the patterns of the emerging unknown?

Early Warning Systems: Seeing and Influencing Patterns During Challenging Times

Patterns that have influenced leadership decisions in the past have included competition, revenue, employee opinion and performance and environmental trends. There are more patterns at play that most don't see because they have been trained to look for what is traditional.

This session will:

- Create an awareness of the shadow patterns that influence environmental, organizational and individual behavior.
- Identify a different way of thinking about patterns.
- Create an understanding of the conditions that shape the speed, path and outcome of a pattern

Dynamical Leadership: Accomplishing What Others Say is Impossible

Dynamical change results from multiple forces acting in unpredictable ways, generating surprising outcomes. The Leadership Landscape Diagram

- Creates an understanding of the forces at play
- Outlines the key factors leaders need to be paying attention to
- Identifies power points that will influence change
- Defines key leadership competencies for leading during times of rapid change

Ray Silverstein

Ray Silverstein is a small business expert, advocate, and author known for his humorous, insightful, business parables and presentations.

Ray has spent decades collecting and studying real-life stories of entrepreneurial success and failure. He has shared many of them in his books, "The Best Secrets of Great Small Business" and "The Small Business Survival Guide." He is an online columnist for the *Phoenix Business Journal* and has contributed numerous articles to *Entrepreneur.com*.

Ray knows a thing or two about success. He has owned, grown, and sold several businesses, including a hand tool manufacturing company and automotive parts company that he grew into multi-million dollar enterprises before divesting them in the 1980s.

Today, Ray talks to hundreds of business professionals each month, discussing every aspect of running and growing a business, from sales and marketing to finance and leadership. One of his favorite expressions is the ancient proverb, *All of Us Are Smarter than One of Us.*

Ray works out of Phoenix and Chicago.

Hot Topics:

What's in the Secret Sauce? – 7 surprise ingredients for success.

The cookie-cutter approach to success doesn't work for every business. In this entrepreneurial seminar, attendees will learn the seven surprise ingredients for creating their own successful "secret sauce," some which include:

- Entrepreneurial DNA
- The Crown Jewels
- The Art of Differentiation

Ready, Set, Grow – Best practices for building successful sales

If sales aren't growing, the company can't either. In this roll-up-your-sleeves workshop, we'll review the best practices for building a successful sales organization. Attendees will learn how to:

- Craft an effective USP (Unique Sales Proposition)
- Define your Sales Funnel to maximize success
- Hire the right kind of salesperson for your organization.
- Taking referrals to a whole new level!

Send Your Sales Skyrocketing – Steps for firing up your sales force, elevating your brand, and landing the customers you want most.

So many companies would like to hit the 'reset' button on sales performance. Invite them to this workshop instead! We'll learn how to give sales operations a step-by-step tune-up that will boost results into overdrive. Topic Areas include...

- Tips for firing up a sales force (no, it isn't about commission!)
- How to elevate your brand
- Smoothing out, and ramping up, your sales process
- Best ways to land the customers you want most

Understanding the Corporate Life Cycle – As companies develop, they face different requirements and challenges. Give your business what it needs to stay healthy at every stage.

As companies develop, they face different requirements and challenges. Whether just starting up or coasting along, companies at every stage will learn how to give their business what it needs now, and it what it will need in the future. We'll discuss:

- Phases of the corporate life cycle (where are you?)
- The benefits and pitfalls of every stage
- Questions you should be asking yourself
- How to stay ahead of the curve

Dr. Terri Trent

Terri Trent is a knowledgeable business focused organizational consultant, executive coach, and facilitator, who specializes in providing innovative business solutions for both organizations and individuals. She has more than twenty years of diverse experience in organizational change, executive coaching, performance management, leadership development, group facilitation, curriculum design, and business communications.

Terri's current focus and specific areas of expertise include executive coaching, assessment of organizational effectiveness, curriculum design using adult learning theory, group facilitation, leadership development, change management, diversity training, team building, competency development, conflict resolution, and multiple assessments, including the StrengthsFinder and Myers-Briggs Type Inventory.

In addition to her current consulting work, Terri is an online graduate instructor in organizational development and human resources management at both DeVry University and the University of Phoenix.

Hot Topics:

Leadership

- Creating an Engaging Workplace: A Guide for Leaders & Managers
- Using Psychological Type and Temperament to Develop and Strengthen Teams

Diversity

- Multiple Generations at Work
- Respecting and Valuing Diversity
- Unlock Your Career Potential by Developing Talents and Strengths

Personal Effectiveness

- The Bounce Back: Developing Resiliency Through the White Waters of Change
- Making Career Connections: Strategies for Managing Your Career in a Changing World of Work

Communication

- Negotiation Strategies that Create a Win-Win Outcome
- Persuasion Strategies for Maximum Impact
- Creative Facilitation Techniques for Trainers and Facilitators
- Emotional Intelligence at Work: Why it is as Important as IQ for Achieving Workplace Success

Elena Zee

 In her eighteen year career, Elena Zee has done business in more than twenty countries, responsible for Risk Management, Portfolio Management, Customer Service and Information Management.

Elena has a Master's Degree in Economics from Columbia University as a President Fellow and Double Bachelor's degrees in Economics and Math from Wellesley College. She was born and raised in Shanghai, China and often coaches individuals and businesses on working with China and understanding people from the Chinese culture.

Elena is on the Board of Arizona Council on Economic Education, Chinese Chamber of Commerce of Arizona, Arizona Humanities Council and Co-President of Phi Beta Kappa Phoenix Association.

Hot Topics:

Win business and work effectively with the Chinese culture

- Chinese history
- Chinese culture vs. American culture
- How to win the Chinese business

Current Affairs and China – open forum discussion

- International Trade
- Human Rights
- Environment and Politics

Chinese Economy

- Centrally planned system vs. free market system
- Labor market
- Housing

Chinese calligraphy and cuisine

- History of the calligraphy and practice
- Introduction to different cuisines
- Cuisine field trip

SPEAKERS RESOURCE ORGANIZATION

SPEAKERS RESOURCE ORGANIZATION

Speakers Resource Organization is a dedicated group of seasoned professionals with a variety of industry backgrounds and expertise who provide thought-provoking presentations and great takeaways. We are proud of the high level of experienced educators and facilitators that we have attracted. We specialize in serving the needs of organizations, business advisory groups, corporations and non-profit groups.

Our goals are to maintain integrity with quality delivery that exceeds client expectations and to engage in generative learning. We are committed to helping create great events through information, sharing and teaching. Looking for a specific topic or time frame? We can assist with either, made to order.

If you or someone you know is interested in becoming a member and has the skills and experience to deliver top-notch presentations, please contact us. Joining SRO will put you in contact not only with organizations, but with professionals who can help you develop your skills as a professional speaker, including a variety of technical services to help your web presence.

We provide 20-, 40- and 60-minute presentations to meet the variety of scheduling needs for your company, group or organization. If you would like to book a speaker, please visit our website and use our **Contact Page**.

On the following pages you will find our speakers' bios, descriptions and a list of hot topics. If you don't see exactly what you are looking for, no doubt our presenters can craft a presentation specifically to your needs. To view individual websites and/or blogs you can visit our **Presenters** page on the website. Visit our website: **www.SpeakersResourceOrganization.com**